Confirmed Bachelors Are Just So Fascinating

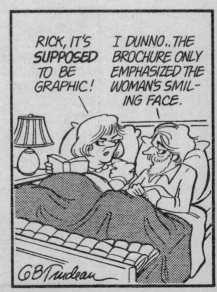

ABOUT
THE
AUTHOR

GARRY TRUDEAU launched his Pulitzer Prize-winning cartoon strip, DOONESBURY in 1970. When he took a leave of absence in December of 1982, the strip was appearing in 710 newspapers in the U.S. and abroad, with an estimated readership of 60 million. His animated film, "A Doonesbury Special," made with John and Faith Hubley for NBC-TV, was nominated for an Academy Award and received the Special Jury Prize at the Cannes Film Festival. His characters have also hit Broadway in the musical "Doonesbury."